# FROM **CANE** TO **SUGAR**

by Jill Braithwaite

Lerner Publications Company / Minneapolis

Text copyright © 2004 by Lerner Publications
Company

Lerner Publications Company
A division of Lerner Publishing Group
241 First Avenue North
Minneapolis, MN 55401 U.S.A.

Website address: www.lernerbooks.com

Library of Congress Cataloging-in-Publication Data

Braithwaite, Jill.
    From cane to sugar / by Jill Braithwaite.
       p.    cm. — (Start to finish)
    Includes index.
    Summary: Briefly introduces the process by which sugar
is made from sugarcane.
    ISBN: 0–8225–0940–7 (lib. bdg. : alk. paper)
    1. Sugar—Manufacture and refining—Juvenile literature.
[1. Sugar.] I. Title. II. Start to finish (Minneapolis, Minn.)
TP378.2 .B73 2004
664'.122—dc21                              2002014356

Manufactured in the United States of America
1 2 3 4 5 6 – DP – 09 08 07 06 05 04

The photographs in this book appear courtesy of:
© Todd Strand/Independent Picture Service, cover,
pp. 3, 23; © John D. Cunningham/Visuals
Unlimited, pp. 1 (top), 5; © Karlene V. Schwartz,
p. 1 (bottom); © Paul Morris/Sugar Cane Growers
Cooperative of Florida, pp. 7, 19; © Trip/H. Rogers,
p. 9; © United States Sugar Corporation, pp. 11,
13, 15, 21; © Mark E. Gibson/Visuals Unlimited,
p. 17

# Table of Contents

# Sugar tastes sweet.

How is it made?

# Farmers grow sugarcane.

Most sugar comes from sugarcane.
Farmers grow this plant just for
making sugar.  Each plant has a
tall, thick cane.  Inside the cane
is a sweet liquid called cane juice.

5

# Farmers cut the sugarcane.

Sugarcane plants grow for about one to two years. Then they are ready to be made into sugar. Farmers use big machines to cut down the cane.

# Machines crush the cane.

Piles of cane are taken to a factory where sugar is made. The cane is put into a machine that has rollers. The rollers squeeze out the cane juice.

9

# The cane juice is heated.

The cane juice is poured into a huge pot called a **vat.** The juice is heated. Heating makes the juice thick, like syrup.

11

# Sugar begins to form.

The syrup is poured into another vat and heated again.  The syrup turns into a thick, brown mixture. Tiny pieces of sugar begin to form in the mixture.  These pieces are called **crystals.**

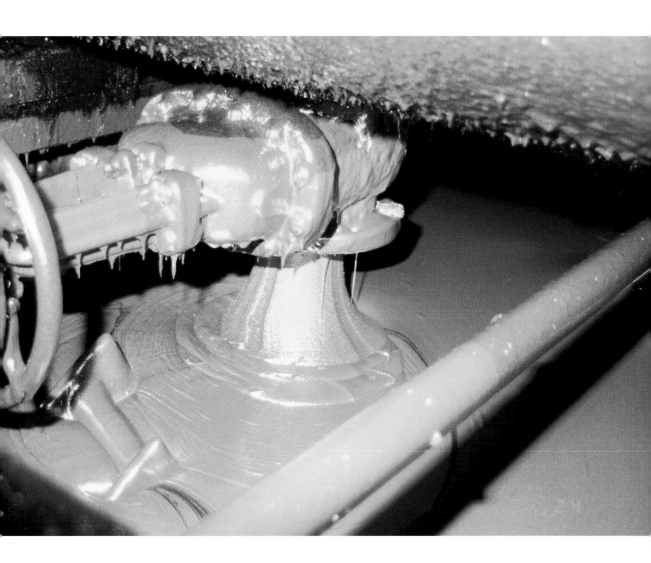

13

# The mixture is spun.

The sugar mixture is put into a machine called a **centrifuge.** Centrifuges spin very fast. The brown sugar crystals stick to the insides of the centrifuge. Leftover mixture drains out the bottom.

A 4

A 5

# The sugar is cleaned.

The brown sugar crystals are sent to a **refinery.** A refinery is a place where sugar is cleaned. The brown color is rinsed off the crystals. Parts that are not good to eat are removed.

# The sugar is dried.

The clean sugar is mixed with water. It is heated and spun again. Tiny white crystals form. The crystals are poured into machines to be dried. Workers move the dried sugar to large rooms to be stored.

# The sugar is sent to factories and stores.

The dried sugar is ready to be used. Some is sent to factories that make food. Some is poured into bags. These packages of sugar are ready to be sent to stores to be sold.

# Enjoy a sweet treat!

You can use sugar in many kinds of foods. Put sugar on your cereal or on a grapefruit. Use sugar to make cookies. It's fun to have a sweet treat!

# Glossary

**centrifuge (SEHN-truh-fyooj):** a machine used to spin sugar

**crystals (KRIHS-tuhlz):** tiny pieces of sugar

**refinery (ree-FY-nur-ee):** a place where sugar is cleaned

**sugarcane (SHU-gur-kayn):** a kind of grass used to make sugar

**vat (VAT):** a large pot

# Index